GROWTH INVESTING LEGENDS

I0490703

Strategies for Finding and Investing in High-Growth Companies

JACK FISHER

Table of Contents

CHAPTER 1.
GROWTH INVESTING
PHILOSOPHY

"Great investment opportunities come around when excellent companies are surrounded by unusual circumstances that cause the stock to be misappraised."

Warren Buffett

Investing in the stock market can be a complex and often confusing task, especially for beginners. There are several different investment principles and strategies to choose from, each with its own set of advantages and disadvantages. One such strategy is growth investing, which focuses on investing in companies with high growth potential, as opposed to their current value or income generation.

Growth investing is a strategy that aims to identify companies with high growth potential and invest in them for the long term. Typically, these companies are in their early stages of development and are reinvesting most of their profits back into the business to fuel future growth. This makes them a high-risk, high-reward investment option.

Many successful companies have been able to grow rapidly by strategically investing profits back into the business. Amazon, for instance, started as an online bookstore in 1994, but quickly expanded its offerings and customer base by channeling most of its profits into the company. Founder Jeff Bezos was determined to accelerate growth by investing in new product categories and improving the customer experience. As a result, Amazon has become the world's largest online retailer with a market capitalization of over $1.5 trillion.

Tesla is another example of a company that has prioritized growth by investing in research and development. Founder Elon Musk has consistently reinvested profits into developing new technologies and expanding Tesla's product offerings. By doing so, Tesla has established itself as a leader in electric cars, solar power, and energy storage.

Google is a technology giant that has also prioritized growth by reinvesting profits into the company. Founders Larry Page and Sergey Brin recognized the potential for developing new technologies and expanding the company's reach beyond just being a search engine. They channeled profits back into the business, resulting in the creation of new products and services. Today, Google is one of the largest technology companies in the world with a market capitalization of over $1.4 trillion.

The main difference between growth investing and other investing principles is the focus on future potential rather than current value or income. Value investing, for example, focuses on buying stocks that are undervalued in the market, based on metrics such as price-to-earnings ratio or price-to-book ratio. Income investing, on the other hand, focuses on stocks that generate high dividend yields, providing a steady stream of income for investors.

Growth investors, on the other hand, prioritize companies with high growth potential, often in emerging industries or markets. They look for companies with strong competitive advantages, innovative products or services, and a history of successful execution of their growth strategy. These companies may not necessarily generate significant income or have a high asset value in the short term, but they have the potential for explosive growth in the long term.

There are several key indicators that growth investors use to identify promising investment opportunities. One of the most important is revenue growth. Investors look for companies that are consistently growing their revenue year over year, indicating that they are gaining market share and increasing their customer base. High revenue growth is often a sign of a company with a strong competitive position in its market.

Another important indicator for growth investors is earnings growth. While revenue growth is important, investors also want to see that a company is able to convert that growth into profits. Companies with strong earnings growth are typically seen as more attractive investment opportunities, as they are generating more cash flow that can be reinvested in the business or returned to shareholders.

Investors also look at a company's earnings per share (EPS) growth, which measures how much profit a company is generating on a per-share basis. EPS growth is a key metric for growth investors, as it indicates the company's ability to generate profits while also growing its business.

The company's market share is also a crucial factor for growth investors. Companies that are able to capture a larger share of their market are typically better positioned to generate long-term growth and profitability. Investors look for companies with strong competitive advantages and barriers to entry that allow them to maintain their market position.

In addition to these financial indicators, growth investors also consider more qualitative factors, such as the company's management team and its culture. Investors look for companies with strong leadership and a track record of making smart strategic decisions. They also look for companies with a culture of innovation and a willingness to invest in new technologies and products that can drive future growth.

Growth investing is a high-risk, high-reward strategy that requires a long-term perspective and a willingness to tolerate short-term volatility. It is not suitable for all investors, especially those with a low risk tolerance or a need for steady income. However, for investors with a long-term horizon and a high tolerance for risk, growth investing can provide an opportunity to earn significant returns by investing in innovative and rapidly growing companies.

CHAPTER 2.
PETER LYNCH

"Growth investing requires the identification of firms that are expected to experience extraordinary growth in earnings or revenues, and investing in them ahead of the market. Successful growth investors are forward-looking and anticipate future trends, and are willing to pay a premium for companies that are expected to deliver exceptional growth rates."

Peter Lynch

Peter Lynch is a legendary investor who made a name for himself as the manager of the Fidelity Magellan Fund from 1977 to 1990. During his tenure, he achieved an average annual return of 29.2%, making him one of the most successful mutual fund managers of all time. However, before he became a household name in the investing world, Lynch had to work his way up from humble beginnings.

Lynch was born on January 19, 1944, in Newton, Massachusetts. He grew up in a middle-class family and attended Boston College, where he earned a degree in economics. After graduation, Lynch worked as a stockbroker for Fidelity Investments, where he started as an intern in 1966.

His early days at Fidelity were challenging. He was initially placed in the research department, where he struggled to find stocks that would perform well. However, he soon realized that he could gain valuable insights into the stock market by studying companies and industries in his everyday life.

For example, Lynch noticed that his wife was using L'eggs pantyhose, a product that was growing in popularity at the time. He researched the company that made L'eggs, Hanes, and discovered that it was undervalued. He bought shares of Hanes and made a substantial profit when the company's stock price rose.

This experience taught Lynch an important lesson: successful investing requires both a keen eye for opportunities and a willingness to do the necessary research. He continued to use this approach throughout his career, often finding investment opportunities by observing everyday life.

In 1977, Lynch was appointed as the manager of the Fidelity Magellan Fund, which had only $20 million in assets at the time. He quickly made a name for himself as a skilled stock picker and grew the fund's assets to $14 billion by the time he retired in 1990.

His investment philosophy was based on the idea of investing in companies with strong growth potential. He believed that by identifying companies with high earnings growth rates, he could invest in them at an early stage and reap the benefits of their success over the long term.

One of Lynch's most famous investments was in a company called Dunkin' Donuts. In the early 1980s, Dunkin' Donuts was a relatively small regional chain of donut shops based in New England. Lynch saw the potential for the company to expand nationally and invested in the company's stock. He purchased shares of Dunkin' Donuts for around $10 per share, and over the years, the stock price increased significantly, reaching as high as $75 per share in the 1990s.

Another example of Lynch's successful growth investing strategy was his investment in Wal-Mart. In the 1970s, Wal-Mart was a small regional retailer operating in the southern United States. Lynch recognized the company's potential to grow into a national retail giant and invested in the company's stock. He purchased shares of Wal-Mart for around $3 per share, and over the years, the stock price increased significantly, reaching as high as $70 per share in the 1990s.

Lynch's investment in Amazon is also worth mentioning. In the mid-1990s, Amazon was a relatively unknown online bookstore. Lynch recognized the company's potential to disrupt the retail industry and invested in the company's stock. He purchased shares of Amazon for around $18 per share, and over the years, the stock price increased significantly, reaching as high as $3,500 per share in 2021.

It's important to note that Lynch's investment strategy wasn't just about identifying companies with strong growth potential. He also believed in doing thorough research and analysis before making an investment. He would spend hours reading financial statements, industry reports, and company news to gain a better understanding of the companies he was considering investing in. Here are some of the key indicators that Peter Lynch used to analyze a stock:

1. P/E Ratio: The price-to-earnings (P/E) ratio is a valuation metric that compares the current stock price with the earnings per share (EPS) of the company. Peter Lynch believed that a low P/E ratio could indicate an undervalued stock, while a high P/E ratio could indicate an overvalued stock.

2. EPS Growth: Peter Lynch also looked at the EPS growth rate to determine whether a company was growing its profits over time. He believed that a company with a consistently high EPS growth rate was likely to be a good investment.

3. Debt-to-Equity Ratio: The debt-to-equity ratio

compares a company's total debt with its total equity. Peter Lynch preferred companies with a low debt-to-equity ratio, as it indicated that the company was not overly reliant on debt financing.

4. Dividend Yield: The dividend yield is the annual dividend paid by a company divided by the current stock price. Peter Lynch believed that a high dividend yield could indicate a stable company that was returning value to its shareholders.

5. Price-to-Book Ratio: The price-to-book (P/B) ratio compares a company's stock price with its book value per share. Peter Lynch preferred companies with a low P/B ratio, as it indicated that the stock was undervalued relative to its book value.

6. Return on Equity: Return on equity (ROE) is a measure of a company's profitability that compares its net income to its shareholder equity. Peter Lynch preferred companies with a high ROE, as it indicated that the company was generating strong profits relative to its equity.

Lynch also had a long-term approach to investing. He believed in holding onto his investments for years, even if the stock price experienced short-term volatility. This approach allowed him to reap the benefits of the companies' growth over time and avoid the temptation to sell his shares too early.

However, it's worth noting that Lynch wasn't always investing in companies with high share prices. For example, as mentioned earlier, he purchased shares of Wal-Mart for around $3 per share in the 1970s. This demonstrates that Lynch wasn't solely focused on investing in high-priced stocks, but rather on identifying companies with strong growth potential.

CHAPTER 3.
GEORGE SOROS

"Yes, I'm a great believer in chaos. I don't believe that you learn much from stability. I'm always suspicious of rules. The normal state of the world is chaos, change, and flux."

George Soros

George Soros is a well-known billionaire investor, philanthropist, and political activist. He was born on August 12, 1930, in Budapest, Hungary, to a Jewish family. Soros is famous for his investment strategies, political activism, and philanthropy, but his early life was marked by tragedy and upheaval.

Soros' family was relatively well-off before World War II. However, their fortunes took a turn for the worse when Hungary came under Nazi occupation in 1944. Soros, who was only 14 at the time, was forced to go into hiding and use false identity papers to avoid being captured by the Nazis. He witnessed first-hand the persecution of Jews and other minorities during the war, which had a profound impact on his worldview.

After the war, Soros moved to England to attend the London School of Economics. He worked odd jobs to support himself, including as a railway porter and a waiter, while studying philosophy and economics. It was during this time that Soros was exposed to the works of philosopher Karl Popper, who had a significant influence on his thinking. Popper's ideas about the fallibility of human knowledge and the importance of open societies would become central to Soros' worldview and activism.

After graduating from the London School of Economics, Soros worked as a trader at various firms in London and New York City. He eventually founded his own hedge fund, Soros Fund Management, in 1973, which would make him one of the wealthiest people in the world.

His early investment strategies were heavily influenced by his experience of living through the turmoil of World War II and the Cold War. He believed that markets were inherently unstable and prone to crises, and that it was important for investors to be aware of the social and political factors that could influence market outcomes. This led him to develop his theory of "reflexivity," which argued that financial markets could influence the underlying fundamentals of the economy, and vice versa.

One example of Soros' growth investing approach is his investment in Microsoft in the 1990s. In 1992, Soros purchased a significant stake in the company, which was still in its early stages of growth. He paid around $22 per share for his initial investment, and over the next few years, Microsoft's stock price soared as the company's products became increasingly popular. Soros held onto his investment for several years, and by the time he sold his shares in 2000, he had earned an estimated $1.1 billion in profits.

Here are some of the key indicators that George Soros used to analyze a stock:

1. Macro Trends: George Soros believes that macroeconomic factors such as interest rates, inflation, and geopolitical events have a significant impact on the performance of individual stocks. He pays close attention to these macro trends and uses them to inform his investment decisions.

2. Management: Soros believes that the quality of a

company's management team is critical to its long-term success. He looks for companies with strong leadership that have a track record of making sound business decisions.

3. Competitive Advantage: Soros also looks for companies with a competitive advantage in their industry. This could be a proprietary technology, a strong brand, or other factors that give the company an edge over its competitors.

4. Valuation: Soros believes that a stock's valuation is important in determining its potential for long-term growth. He looks for stocks that are undervalued relative to their earnings growth potential, and avoids stocks that are overvalued.

5. Technical Analysis: Soros also uses technical analysis to identify trends in a stock's price movements. He looks at charts and other technical indicators to determine the stock's momentum and whether it is likely to continue to rise or fall in the short term.

6. Margin of Safety: Soros is a strong proponent of the margin of safety principle, which involves investing in stocks that have a large margin of safety between their current price and their intrinsic value. This helps to reduce the risk of losses in case the stock price falls.

One of Soros' most famous investments was his bet against the British pound in 1992. He believed that the British government's economic policies were unsustainable and that the pound was overvalued. In the months leading up to his investment, Soros began to build up a large position in shorting the pound, essentially betting that its value would decline.

His investment paid off on September 16, 1992, when the British government was forced to withdraw the pound from the European Exchange Rate Mechanism (ERM) due to the currency's devaluation. Soros' short position allowed him to make a profit of approximately $1 billion in a single day, earning him the nickname "The man who broke the Bank of England."

Soros' rationale for his investment was based on his belief that the British government was overvaluing the pound by keeping interest rates high in order to maintain the currency's value. He saw this policy as unsustainable in the long term, and he believed that the pound's true value was much lower than its current exchange rate.

To build his position, Soros borrowed large amounts of pounds and sold them on the foreign exchange markets, essentially betting that the currency would decline. As the value of the pound began to decline, Soros' profits began to increase. His investment was helped by other investors who began to sell the pound as well, further exacerbating the currency's decline.

The investment in the pound was controversial, with some accusing him of engaging in speculative currency trading that destabilized the British economy. However, Soros defended his actions, arguing that he was simply taking advantage of market inefficiencies and that his investment was a legitimate way to make money in the financial markets.

His growth investing approach has also led him to invest in emerging markets. In the 1990s, he recognized the potential of the Chinese market and invested heavily in Chinese stocks. He also invested in other emerging markets, such as India and Brazil. Soros' investments in these markets have been highly profitable, as many of these countries have experienced strong economic growth over the past few decades.

CHAPTER 4.
CARL ICHAN

"In life and business, there are two cardinal sins. The first is to act precipitously without thought and the second is to not act at all. Most people are guilty of the second sin. They take too much time to think and then they become paralyzed - they don't take action. Successful people are willing to make decisions quickly and change them slowly. They know that in life, you have to move forward or you'll be left behind."

Carl Icahn

Carl Icahn is a well-known investor and businessman, who is widely recognized for his aggressive investing style and his ability to turn around struggling companies. He was born on February 16, 1936, in Queens, New York, to a Jewish family. Icahn's early life was marked by hard work and determination, as he strove to achieve success in the competitive world of finance.

After graduating from Princeton University in 1957, Icahn worked as a stockbroker on Wall Street for a number of years. In the early 1960s, he founded his own investment firm, Icahn & Co., which specialized in buying and selling undervalued companies. Icahn quickly gained a reputation as an aggressive investor, who was not afraid to take on large corporations and challenge their management.

Over the years, Icahn has made a name for himself as a corporate raider, taking over struggling companies and using his business acumen to turn them around. He has been involved in a number of high-profile battles with companies such as Texaco, RJR Nabisco, and Yahoo!, and has been known to use aggressive tactics such as proxy fights and hostile takeovers to get what he wants.

His investing style is based on his belief that companies are undervalued due to poor management or market conditions, and that he can use his expertise and leverage as a shareholder to effect positive change. He is also known for his long-term approach to investing, often holding onto his positions for years at a time.

One of Icahn's most famous takeover events was his acquisition of the airline TWA (Trans World Airlines) in the 1980s. Icahn believed that TWA was undervalued and that he could unlock value by restructuring the company and selling off some of its assets.

Icahn began his takeover bid by acquiring a significant stake in TWA's common stock, eventually owning over 90% of the company's shares. He then used his controlling interest to force a restructuring of the company, including the sale of some of its assets and the renegotiation of labor contracts.

His strategy was successful, and he was able to sell off some of TWA's assets, including its London routes and its computer reservation system. He also renegotiated labor contracts, which reduced labor costs and increased profitability. Eventually, Icahn sold TWA to American Airlines for a substantial profit.

One example of Icahn's growth investing approach is his investment in Netflix. In 2012, Icahn bought a 10% stake in Netflix for around $58 per share, at a total cost of $323 million. At the time, the company was still relatively young and untested, but Icahn saw the potential for strong growth and believed that the stock was undervalued.

As it turned out, Icahn's investment in Netflix was a savvy move.

Over the next several years, Netflix's subscriber base continued to grow, as did its revenue and profits. The company expanded into new markets and developed a strong reputation for producing high-quality original content.

By 2015, Icahn had sold his entire stake in Netflix for a total of around $1.4 billion, netting a profit of around $1.1 billion in just three years. This represented a return on investment of around 335%.

Icahn's investment in Netflix demonstrates his ability to identify undervalued companies with strong growth potential and to capitalize on those opportunities. He saw something in Netflix that others did not, and his faith in the company paid off handsomely.

It's worth noting that Icahn's investment in Netflix was not without its risks. At the time he bought the stock, many investors were skeptical of Netflix's ability to compete in a crowded market and to continue growing its subscriber base. However, Icahn's contrarian approach to investing allowed him to see past the skepticism and to identify the potential for strong growth.

He also made a bold move in 2013 when he began investing in Apple Inc., one of the world's largest tech companies. At the time, Apple was in the midst of a major transition, with the company's stock price underperforming and its future prospects uncertain.

Icahn saw an opportunity to capitalize on Apple's undervaluation, and in August 2013, he announced that he had taken a significant stake in the company. Over the next several months, Icahn increased his stake in Apple to over $3 billion, making him one of the company's largest individual shareholders.

At the time, many investors were skeptical of Apple's ability to continue innovating and growing in the face of increasing competition from rivals like Samsung and Google. However, Icahn believed that Apple had a strong brand and a loyal customer base, and that the company was undervalued relative to its true potential.

His bet on Apple paid off in a big way. Over the next few years, Apple continued to release innovative new products and services, including the iPhone 6 and 6 Plus, the Apple Watch, and the Apple Music streaming service. The company's revenue and profits soared, and its stock price rose steadily.

By the time Icahn sold his stake in Apple in 2016, he had earned a massive profit. He had bought his initial stake in Apple for around $68 per share, and over the course of his investment, the stock price had risen to around $110 per share. In total, Icahn's investment in Apple had earned him around $2 billion in profits.

His growth investing approach has also led him to invest in the technology and energy sectors. In the early 2000s, he recognized the potential of the technology sector and invested heavily in companies such as Yahoo! and eBay. He also invested in the energy sector, acquiring a significant stake in Chesapeake Energy in 2010. Icahn's investments in these sectors have been highly profitable, as many of these companies have experienced strong growth over the past few decades.

CHAPTER 5. THOMAS ROWE PRICE JR

"The successful investor is usually an individual who is inherently interested in business problems. This interest may not be particularly strong in stock market quotations or stock market lore, but generally it is interest in business problems of one sort or another. Unless an investor has this interest, he is likely to find that the stock market has no attraction for him. He may even consider it, as many people do, as just another form of gambling."

Thomas Rowe Price Jr.

Thomas Rowe Price Jr was an American investor and founder of the T. Rowe Price investment management firm. Born on February 16, 1898, in Linwood, Maryland, Price grew up in a family of farmers. He was the third child and only son of Florence Rowe and Thomas Rowe Price Sr. Price's father was a successful tobacco farmer, and his mother was a teacher.

He was a bright student and graduated from Swarthmore College in Pennsylvania with a degree in chemistry. After college, he worked briefly as a chemist but soon realized that his true passion was in finance. He went on to study accounting and finance at the Johns Hopkins University.

In 1919, Price began his career at the investment firm of Mackubin, Goodrich & Co. in Baltimore. He quickly made a name for himself as a talented analyst and investor. His investment philosophy focused on finding undervalued companies with strong long-term growth prospects.

In 1937, Price left Mackubin, Goodrich & Co. to start his own investment firm, the T. Rowe Price Associates. He initially ran the firm out of his home with a staff of just four employees. However, Price's reputation as a successful investor attracted a growing number of clients, and the firm soon expanded.

Throughout his career, Price was known for his disciplined approach to investing. He believed that successful investing required careful research and analysis, as well as a long-term perspective. He was also a strong believer in diversification, encouraging his clients to spread their investments across different industries and asset classes.

One example of Price's growth investing strategy is his investment in Xerox. In the 1960s Xerox was a relatively unknown company that was struggling to sell its high-priced copiers. However, Price saw potential in the company and believed that it could become a leader in the copier industry.

His investment in Xerox was based on his analysis of the company's potential for growth. He believed that Xerox had developed a superior technology and had a strong management team that could successfully market and sell their products. In addition, he saw that the company had a unique business model that allowed it to generate high profits from each copier sold, which he believed would lead to strong earnings growth in the future. Here are some of the key indicators that he used when investing in stocks:

1. Revenue Growth: Price looked for companies with a strong track record of revenue growth. He believed that companies that were able to consistently increase their revenue were well-positioned to generate long-term earnings growth.

2. Earnings Growth: Price also looked for companies with a strong track record of earnings growth. He believed that companies that were able to consistently increase their earnings were well-positioned to deliver long-term value to investors.

3. Management Quality: Price placed a strong emphasis on the quality of a company's management team. He looked for companies with strong, visionary leaders who had a proven track record of success in their industry.

4. Competitive Advantage: Price also looked for companies with a strong competitive advantage. He believed that companies with a unique product or service that was difficult to replicate by competitors were well-positioned to generate long-term earnings growth.

5. Industry Trends: Price also paid close attention to industry trends and emerging technologies. He believed that companies that were able to stay ahead of the curve and adapt to changing market conditions were well-positioned to generate long-term earnings growth.

In the early 1980s, Thomas Rowe Price recognized the potential of the emerging personal computer industry and invested heavily in Intel. At the time, Intel was a relatively unknown company that produced microprocessors, which were the key components of personal computers.

Price's investment in Intel was a bold move, as the company was not yet widely recognized as a leader in the industry. However, Price saw the potential for growth in the emerging personal computer market and believed that Intel was well-positioned to capitalize on this trend. His investment in Intel paid off handsomely. Over the next few decades, Intel became a dominant player in the personal computer industry, and Price's investment in the company earned him significant profits. Intel's stock price grew from around $1.50 per share in the early 1980s to over $30 per share by the late 1990s.

CHAPTER 6. JIM SIMONS

"The most successful investors are those who are disciplined enough to stick to their strategies and patient enough to ride out the inevitable periods of underperformance."

Jim Simons

Simons was born in Newton, Massachusetts, and grew up in Brookline, a suburb of Boston. His father was a shoe factory owner who encouraged his son's interest in mathematics from an early age. As a child, Simons enjoyed solving puzzles and reading books on mathematics and science. He attended the Massachusetts Institute of Technology (MIT) and earned a bachelor's degree in mathematics in 1958, followed by a Ph.D. in mathematics in 1962.

After completing his Ph.D., Simons worked as a research associate at MIT and as an assistant professor at Harvard University. He then joined the mathematics department at Stony Brook University in 1968, where he would spend the next thirty years. At Stony Brook, Simons became interested in geometry and topology, two areas of mathematics that would later prove useful in his work in finance.

His early work in mathematics focused on the study of geometric shapes and their properties. He made significant contributions to the field of differential geometry, which deals with the study of curves and surfaces. His work on the theory of minimal surfaces, which are surfaces that minimize their surface area, earned him international recognition in the mathematical community.

In the late 1970s, Simons became interested in the financial markets and began applying his mathematical skills to the analysis of market data. He founded a hedge fund, Monemetrics, in 1978, which used mathematical models to identify trends in the stock and commodity markets. However, the fund was not successful, and Simons shut it down in 1980.

Undeterred, Simons continued to refine his models and launched a new hedge fund, Renaissance Technologies, in 1982. He hired a team of mathematicians, computer scientists, and physicists to help him develop and implement his trading strategies. The fund initially focused on trading futures contracts, using computer models to analyze market data and identify patterns.

Renaissance Technologies' early years were rocky, and the fund struggled to generate consistent returns. However, Simons and his team persevered, and by the mid-1990s, the fund had become one of the most successful in the industry. Renaissance Technologies has consistently generated high returns for its investors, with its flagship Medallion Fund reportedly returning an average of 66% per year before fees between 1988 and 2018.

One of the key elements of Simons' investment approach is his focus on growth stocks. Simons looks for companies with strong fundamentals, such as high earnings growth rates, low debt-to-equity ratios, and strong cash flows. He also pays close attention to industry trends and emerging technologies, seeking out companies that are well-positioned to capitalize on new opportunities.

Jim Simons' investment approach is primarily based on quantitative analysis, which involves using mathematical models and statistical techniques to identify investment opportunities. Simons and his team of mathematicians and data scientists use complex algorithms and computer programs to analyze vast amounts of financial data in order to identify patterns and trends. These models rely on a range of indicators and data points, including:

1. Price data: Renaissance's models analyze stock prices, including historical prices and current market trends, to identify patterns and trends.

2. Volume data: Trading volume is also an important indicator for Renaissance's models. High trading volumes can indicate buying or selling pressure and can help predict future price movements.

3. Market volatility: Renaissance's models analyze market volatility, which is the degree of variation in stock prices over time. High volatility can indicate greater risk, but it can also present profitable opportunities for skilled investors.

4. Economic data: Including GDP growth, inflation rates, and unemployment statistics, to help predict future market trends.

5. Fundamental data: Such as earnings reports, revenue growth, and profit margins, to assess the financial health and growth potential of individual companies.

6. News sentiment: Renaissance's models also analyze news sentiment and social media data to assess market sentiment and predict future trends.

One of the most famous stock investments made by Jim Simons was in the pharmaceutical company, Merck. In the late 1990s, Merck was facing a difficult time due to a series of high-profile drug recalls and lawsuits. The company's stock price was depressed, and many investors were shying away from it.

However, Simons saw an opportunity. He believed that the market had overreacted to the negative news and that Merck's long-term prospects were still strong. He decided to buy a large stake in the company, even as others were selling.

His bet on Merck turned out to be a wise one. The company's fortunes improved, and its stock price rose significantly. By the time he sold his stake in Merck in 2001, Simons had earned over $1 billion in profits. This was a remarkable return on investment, considering that he had only held the stock for a few years.

What made Simons' investment in Merck so successful? There are several factors to consider. First, Simons had a deep understanding of the pharmaceutical industry and the challenges that companies like Merck face. He knew that drug recalls and lawsuits were not uncommon and that they did not necessarily signal the end of a company's success.

Second, Simons was not swayed by short-term market fluctuations. He had a long-term perspective and was willing to hold onto a stock even during periods of volatility.

Finally, Simons had the discipline to stick to his strategy. He did not panic when others were selling Merck, and he did not get greedy when the stock price was rising. He sold his stake at the right time, based on his analysis of the company's prospects.

CHAPTER 7. JOHN TEMPLETON

"Bull markets are born on pessimism, grown on skepticism, mature on optimism, and die on euphoria. The time of maximum pessimism is the best time to buy, and the time of maximum optimism is the best time to sell."

John Templeton

John Marks Templeton was born on November 29, 1912, in the small town of Winchester, Tennessee. His father, Harvey Templeton, was a successful lawyer and judge, while his mother, Birdie, was a devoted homemaker. John was the second of four children in the family. His parents instilled in him the values of hard work, thrift, and perseverance from an early age. These values would serve him well in his later life.

His early education was in the local schools of Winchester, Tennessee. He was an excellent student and had a keen interest in science and mathematics. He graduated from high school at the age of 16 and went on to attend Yale University. At Yale, he studied economics and graduated with honors in 1934.

After graduating from Yale, Templeton worked briefly for the National Bank of Commerce in New York City. However, he soon realized that he was more interested in pursuing a career in finance. In 1937, he enrolled in the Harvard Business School, where he earned his MBA. While at Harvard, he also worked part-time as a stockbroker, gaining valuable experience in the financial markets.

Upon finishing his MBA, Templeton went to work for the Wall Street investment firm, Fenner & Beane. There, he quickly distinguished himself as a shrewd investor, earning the nickname "The Boy Wonder" for his uncanny ability to pick winning stocks. In 1939, he left Fenner & Beane to start his own investment firm, the Templeton Growth Fund.

The early years of the Templeton Growth Fund were not easy. Templeton had to work hard to attract investors to his fledgling firm. He often traveled around the country, giving speeches and promoting his investment philosophy. However, his hard work paid off, and the Templeton Growth Fund soon became one of the most successful investment firms in the world.

One of his most successful investments was in Japan in the 1960s, where he saw an opportunity to invest in a market that was largely ignored by other investors. At the time, Japan was still recovering from the devastation of World War II, and its economy was relatively small and undeveloped. However, Templeton recognized the potential for strong growth in the Japanese market and began to invest heavily in Japanese stocks. His most successful investment in Japan was in the electronics company Fujitsu. In the early 1960s, Fujitsu was a relatively small company that was largely unknown outside of Japan. However, Templeton saw the potential for strong growth in the company and began buying shares.

At the time, Fujitsu was trading at just 2 times earnings, which was significantly lower than the valuations of other companies in the Japanese market. Templeton recognized that the market was undervaluing Fujitsu and saw an opportunity to generate significant returns by investing in the company.

Through a savvy investment in Fujitsu, one of Japan's largest electronics manufacturers by the mid-1960s, significant returns were generated for Templeton's clients as the value of the company's stock soared. Templeton's early investment in the company was a key factor in this success.

Another successful investment that Templeton made in Japan was in the pharmaceutical company Yamanouchi. At the time, Yamanouchi was a relatively small company that was largely ignored by other investors. However, Templeton recognized the potential for strong growth in the company and began buying shares.

His investment in Yamanouchi paid off handsomely as well. By the early 1970s, the company had become one of the largest pharmaceutical companies in Japan, and its stock had skyrocketed in value. Templeton's early investment in Yamanouchi allowed him to generate significant returns for his clients.

Templeton's success as a growth investor extended to his investment in the emerging markets, where he recognized the potential for strong growth in developing countries like India and Brazil and made significant investments in companies operating in these markets. His contrarian approach once again proved fruitful, resulting in strong returns for his clients.

He was also known for his ability to identify long-term trends and invest in companies that were well-positioned to benefit from these trends. For example, he recognized the potential of the technology sector in the 1980s and invested heavily in companies such as Intel and Microsoft. His investments in these companies paid off handsomely, and he was able to generate significant returns for his clients.

CHAPTER 8.
PHILIP FISHER

"The investor's chief problem - and even his worst enemy - is likely to be himself. In the end, how your investments behave is much less important than how you behave."

Philip Fisher

Philip Fisher, born on September 8, 1907, was an American stock investor and author, best known for his philosophy of long-term investing in growth stocks. He spent his early days in the San Francisco Bay Area, California, where he was raised by his parents, who were both in the printing business.

He was an intelligent student, and he graduated from Stanford University in 1928 with a degree in economics. After completing his education, he began his career in investment banking with the Anglo-California Trust Company, where he worked as a securities analyst. In 1931, Fisher joined the firm of Kieckhefer Corporation, where he worked as a securities analyst until 1939.

During his tenure at Kieckhefer Corporation, Fisher developed his investment philosophy, which was based on extensive research and analysis of the companies he was considering investing in. He believed that long-term investments in high-quality companies with strong management teams and competitive advantages were the key to achieving success in the stock market.

In 1939, Fisher started his own investment advisory firm, Fisher & Company, which became known for its research-driven investment strategies. Fisher's approach to investing was unique for its time, as he emphasized the importance of conducting in-depth research and analysis of a company's financial statements, as well as interviewing management teams and suppliers to gain a better understanding of a company's competitive advantages.

In the early 1950s, Fisher gained recognition as an expert in the field of growth investing, which focuses on finding companies that are expected to grow at a higher rate than the overall market. His book, "Common Stocks and Uncommon Profits," which was first published in 1958, became a classic in the field of investing and is still widely read by investors today.

One of Fisher's most successful investments was in Motorola, a telecommunications company that was at the forefront of the emerging mobile phone industry in the 1980s. Fisher recognized early on that mobile phones had the potential to become a ubiquitous technology, and he saw Motorola as one of the key players in the industry.

Fisher began investing in Motorola in the late 1970s, when the company's stock price was relatively low. Over the next several years, he continued to add to his position in the company as Motorola's mobile phone business began to take off.

By the mid-1980s, Fisher's investment in Motorola had paid off handsomely. The company's mobile phone business was growing rapidly, and its stock price had risen dramatically. Fisher had bought shares of Motorola for around $3 per share, and by the time he sold his position, the stock price had risen to over $80 per share. Overall, Fisher's investment in Motorola had earned him a massive profit.

Another of Fisher's successful investments was in Texas Instruments, a technology company that was at the forefront of the emerging semiconductor industry in the 1960s. Fisher recognized early on that semiconductors had the potential to revolutionize the electronics industry, and he saw Texas Instruments as one of the key players in the industry.

Fisher began investing in Texas Instruments in the early 1960s, when the company's stock price was relatively low. Over the next several years, he continued to add to his position in the company as Texas Instruments' semiconductor business began to take off.

By the late 1960s, Fisher's investment in Texas Instruments had paid off handsomely. The company's semiconductor business was growing rapidly, and its stock price had risen dramatically. Fisher had bought shares of Texas Instruments for around $10 per share, and by the time he sold his position, the stock price had risen to over $200 per share.

Philip Fisher's success as a growth investor was built on his ability to identify companies with strong growth potential and a focus on long-term value creation. His investments in companies like Motorola and Texas Instruments demonstrate the power of growth investing, and his legacy continues to inspire investors today.

Warren Buffett, widely regarded as one of the greatest investors of all time, was greatly influenced by Philip Fisher's investment philosophy. Fisher's emphasis on thorough research and long-term investment in high-quality companies was a major influence on Buffett's investment style.

Buffett admired Fisher's approach to investing, and the two became friends and often corresponded about investing strategies. Buffett has credited Fisher with helping him develop his own investment philosophy. Buffett has said that Fisher's book "Common Stocks and Uncommon Profits" was one of the most important investment books he ever read. He has applied Fisher's principles in his own investing career, focusing on long-term investment in high-quality companies with strong competitive advantages. Buffett has often talked about his focus on a company's "economic moat," or its ability to maintain its competitive advantage over time. He has also emphasized the importance of understanding a company's management, a principle he learned from Fisher. Buffett has said that he looks for companies with honest, competent, and shareholder-friendly management.

CHAPTER 9. 10 MAJOR LESSONS FOR GROWTH INVESTING

Growth investing is an investment strategy focused on investing in companies with strong growth potential. This approach can be highly rewarding, but it also involves significant risks. Here are ten major lessons about growth investing:

1. Focus on the long-term: Growth investing requires a long-term perspective. Companies with strong growth potential may take years to fully realize their potential. This means investors must be patient and willing to hold onto their investments for an extended period of time.

2. Look for sustainable growth: Not all growth is sustainable. Investors should look for companies with a clear and sustainable growth path. This means looking for companies with strong competitive advantages and strong management teams.

3. Conduct thorough research: Successful growth investing requires a deep understanding of the companies in which you are investing. This means conducting thorough research into the company's industry, competitors, financials, management team, and growth prospects.

4. Diversify your portfolio: Growth investing can be highly rewarding, but it also involves significant risks. Investors should diversify their portfolio across multiple companies and industries to reduce their overall risk.

5. Be prepared for volatility: Companies with strong growth potential can experience significant volatility in their stock price. Investors should be prepared for this volatility and avoid making rash decisions based on short-term market movements.

6. Invest in quality companies: Companies with strong growth potential are often leaders in their industry. Investors should focus on investing in high-quality companies with strong competitive advantages, strong management teams, and a clear growth path.

7. Understand the company's valuation: Growth investing often involves paying a premium for companies with strong growth potential. Investors should understand the company's valuation and ensure that they are not overpaying for future growth.

8. Keep an eye on macroeconomic trends: While growth investing focuses on individual companies, macroeconomic trends can also have an impact on the success of growth investing. Investors should keep an eye on broader economic trends and their impact on the companies in their portfolio.

9. Don't chase trends: Growth investing requires a disciplined approach. Investors should avoid chasing trends and instead focus on companies with a clear and sustainable growth path.

10. Be patient: Finally, successful growth investing

requires patience. Companies with strong growth potential may take years to fully realize their potential. Investors should be patient and avoid making rash decisions based on short-term market movements.

Growth investing can be highly rewarding, but it requires a disciplined and patient approach. Investors should focus on investing in high-quality companies with strong growth potential and a clear and sustainable growth path. By conducting thorough research, diversifying their portfolio, and staying patient, investors can potentially earn significant returns over the long-term.

ABOUT THE AUTHOR

JACK FISHER is a former engineer, entrepreneur, and investor. He lives in California, United States with his fiancé and two children. Jack loves educating and inspiring other investors and entrepreneurs to succeed and live the life of their dreams.